## Introductio

This book will cover in as much detail ⟨ within the following boundaries:–

The northern boundary will be the railv ⟩ ......... ⟩ ɪɪɔɪɪɪ ʌʌɪɪɪ ɪɪɪ Eastern Road to the railway bridge on the Northern Road at Cosham. West will be the Northern Road from that railway bridge to Portsbridge. The eastern will be from the railway bridge on the Eastern Road to the southern end of the water bridge on the same road. The southern will be and will include Portscreek.

Although the central theme will be the Highbury Estate the remainder of the area merits including as the recreational and play areas of several generations of Highbury residents.

As is our usual policy we will go back as far as possible with the stories and information coming up to around 1960.

The cover design is taken from Mitchell's original advert for the estate houses whilst the full advert can be seen below.

## Forward

With the exception of the area immediately bordering Cosham railway station the entire locality up to around 1930 was basically open land. It was split into three easily definable sections as follows: East Cosham Marshes, the Railway Triangle and what was to become the Highbury Estate. Portscreek will be dealt with separately.

Maps of the middle 1800's show the area to be devoid of anything apart from a small building which stood approximately where numbers 125–137 Hawthorn Crescent now stand (see Highbury section). This was probably the cottage which stood till around 1958 in the midst of modern housing. The same building appears on the 1870 map as Little Salterns and has been joined by Hawthorn Cottage and Portsbridge Cottages.

By 1938 the area had been developed into the form which it was to stay basically unaltered to the end of our self imposed period with the major exception of about 100 pre-fabs built in the immediate post-war years. The other major project was the Eastern Road which although it forms our eastern boundary forms no part of this book, although a brief description of the water bridge construction is given in the appropriate section. The war brought few changes to the area and while some signs of it have remained even to the present day, most had gone by 1960. All of these will be dealt with in their respective sections.

One remaining small area that will be looked at in its own right will be the area bounded by Northern and Portsmouth Roads and the railway line at Cosham.

We hope that you, the reader, will enjoy this book and bear with us in any small errors made but we also hope that anything that you consider to be definitely wrong will be pointed out to us so that it can be rectified for future use.

*Malcolm Garlick*

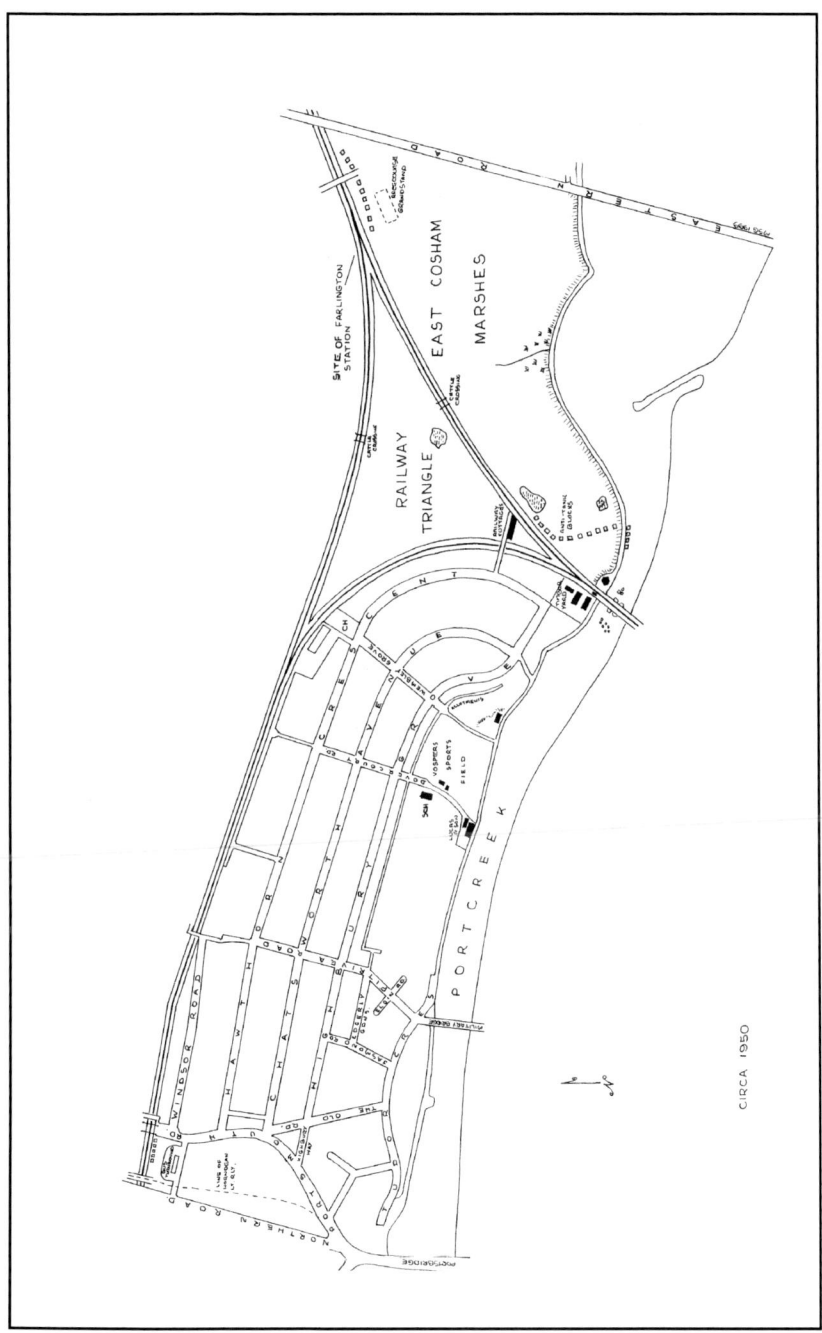

## Section One – East Cosham Marshes

Basically a triangle of land formed by the railway, the Eastern Road and the creek. In its early days it was prone to flooding with the tides and remained so until the building of the embankment by Mitchell's in the 1930's. Apparently there was a proposition to carry the estate onto this area via a continuation of Highbury Grove and a bridge over the railway but the council withheld planning permission. This may account for the embankment being a half-hearted affair compared with the section between the railway bridge and Portsbridge. On one occasion in the 1930's floods reached well up into Station Road which would be something in the region of half a mile from the present shoreline. The embankment itself consisted of clay built-up and sloping downward on the landward side, whilst that facing the water was made of wooden stakes with a loose hardcore infill and the whole topped off by grass. Although basically successful the area still suffered localised shallow flooding despite the many drainage ditches throughout its life. The area never appeared to be used for anything apart from grazing cattle and was in the main just left to nature.

In the 1950's it had two good ponds (the smaller of which would often dry up in summer) which were well stocked with frogs and newts. Bushes full of birds' nests with Blackbirds, Song Thrushes and Hedge Sparrows being rife, with Moorhens in the large ponds and such rarities as the Dartford Warbler and an oddity (for this area) in the form of a Partridge which on one occasion laid a clutch of 16 eggs. There was a least one foxes earth – unusual for that time but definitely not today. Cows were often in residence as were on some occasions, a few horses, although where they came from I do not know. There is a possibility that they came from a farm at the bottom of Lower Drayton Lane and across the cattle crossing on the railway on the north side of the railway triangle. From there they would have gone across the other crossing on the eastern side of the triangle and onto the marshes. If anyone can confirm this I would like to hear from them.

The railway arrived in 1847 and effectively isolated the area from the developing areas of Drayton and Cosham. Although it was the main line into Portsmouth for the London, Brighton and South Coast Railway (L.B.& S.C.R.) and obviously saw a lot of use, as far as I am aware it only suffered one major accident in our area. This occurred in 1894 when a Farlington bound train was passing through Farlington Station and the leading van left the rails. The result was a considerable amount of damage to both train and station and the unfortunate death of the guard and injury to eight passengers. Farlington Station was opened in 1891 to accommodate the crowds that flocked to Farlington (horse) Race Course. Although the Grandstand and some of the tack impinged onto this area the majority of the course was on Farlington Marshes and is not dealt with here. A picture of the Grandstand can be found in 'Portsmouth in Old Picture Postcards' by Messrs. Francis and Rogers. The racecourse and a lot of Farlington Marshes was taken over by the army during WWI and the course was never re-opened after the war. The Grandstand was demolished and the station downgraded to Halt status and ceased to exist as such in the late 1930's. It was definitely in use in 1936/7 as one of our contributors used to catch the train to Portsmouth at a cost of 4d return. Following WWII some attempts were made to re-open the halt to cater for the industrial development in the immediate area but although a spur existed for the Co-op depots to the north of the line these efforts remained stillborn. Traces of the platforms in the form of grass covered humps remained in evidence well into the 50's and probably beyond. The railway carried on to Portscreek Junction where it crossed the creek originally on a wooden bridge. This was replaced in 1910 by a substantial structure which, as far as railways in this country are concerned, to say the least was unusual. It was built as a drawbridge raised by something akin to sheerlegs and when raised gave access to Naval and other vessels using the creek as well as cutting access to the island by any unwelcome visitors. This access requirement had been insisted on by the military in order to keep the defences of Portsmouth secure from the landward side. In the following years the need for such security measures disappeared and the bridge was fixed. I have found no evidence apart from the original trials of the bridge ever being used in the lift mode. The railway, although originally a steam line, was electrified under the ownership of the Southern Railway and saw very little steam haulage after. One or two freight trains and the occasional 'special' but the most regular steamer was the 'Hayling Billy' going from its home at Fratton to Havant for its days' duty on the Hayling Island Branch and back to Fratton at night.

Although the Eastern Road existed from Velder Avenue to just south of Portscreek in 1939, it went no further. The water bridge was started in 1939 with Parkes of Portsmouth delivering the first item of building equipment in the form of a large crane. This was driven down from London by Mr. Cyril Stares and delivered to the south shore of the creek via Tangiers Road. The actual construction was carried out by McAlpines. The bridge itself was built from the land outwards using the crane and simultaneously from the water inwards using a barge fitted with pile driving equipment. It is probable that, as the barge was apparently quite old, it finally sank where it had been working and was just left to rot away. Finally the causeways from the land to the bridge were filled in and the road surfaced.

During the war, passes were issued if you had to use the bridge. It could be crossed on foot long before it was finished but it was too rough to cycle on. My father worked at Airspeeds and lived at Farlington and came home at dinner time. This meant he had to cross the bridge and carry his bike some of the way four times a day. He was extremely pleased when it was completed.

To facilitate the building of the causeway between the water and railway bridges across the very boggy land, chalk was brought from Farlington Redoubt and down Station Road. At the bottom of the road where the railway had to be crossed a temporary bridge was erected by the army. Although it was always known as a Bailey Bridge there is some doubt as to the accuracy of this statement. The other name is a Callender Hamilton Bridge. Having recently unearthed some period pictures of the former I feel that the latter description is correct. The bridge stayed at the site till about 1960 when it was taken down and re-erected in a different form over the railway at Rat Lane (Norway Road). In its original form it was straight but when at Rat Lane was in the form of a squared U. Once the causeway had been built the railway bridge could be started. The run-ups either side were built using rubble from either bombed or demolished buildings in the city. As far as I am aware, McAlpines had no part in the construction of this bridge. The last part of the road was built from the railway northwards and from Havant Road southwards at the same time. I do not know its official date of completion but it was in regular use by 1945. During the war it was used as an operating point for smoke generators but with the prevailing SW wind their use must have been somewhat restricted.

The war brought about minor defence works in the form of a pillbox and two rows of anti-tank blocks. The latter weighed approximately 2.5 tons each and had four steel bars sticking out of the top. These were liberally wrapped in barbed wire which was, painfully, still there up to the time of their clearance around the late 1960's. The pillbox still exists adjacent to Portscreek railway bridge.

*Anti-tank blocks*

There was a well defined track that went from near the SW corner of the area and went in a NW direction towards the Eastern Road. It was made from compressed cinders and brick rubble and had probably been used in building the defences although it had existed as a track on a much smaller scale long before that. Its original use must stay as pure conjecture. The area was probably used during the war for training purposes (probably the Home Guard) as several military bits and pieces came to light during the 1950's including a bayonet which, although rusty, was in quite good condition.

## Section Two – The Railway Triangle

As its name suggests, this was a triangle of land bounded on all sides by the railway. To the east was the L.B. & S.C.R. opened in 1847, with the north and west sides edged by the L.S.W.R. which were both opened in 1848. The northern link between the two independent systems never saw anything like the usage that the other two lines had but it did give the advantage of being able to travel along the south coast without having to make a detour into Portsmouth.

The enclosed land saw very little use right up to the 1970's when it finally succumbed to the developer. Until than it was only used sparsely for grazing cattle and in the 50's and 60's it was often the home of a very belligerent horse whose main enjoyment in life seemed to be chasing groups of youngsters coming back from the marshes the long way round. The usual reason for them using this route was because the tide was too high to walk under the railway bridge. The field itself was just open ground with a few bushes and a pond. Cattle crossings were to be found on the north and east railway lines and adjacent to the one on the north were traces of what could have been old cattle pens or the like. At this point were also a few tall trees complete with a rookery.

The southern point of the triangle was used by the railway as a small housing area for its employees. The houses were six in number and built in blocks of two. I believe they were built around the turn of the century and were to the standards of the day but with the bonus of small gardens at the back and front. The very point of the triangle was given over to allotments for the occupants and from memory they were fairly productive. The houses had gravel paths back and front and were connected to Hawthorn Crescent by means of an iron bridge over the railway. Boards were laid between the lines to enable the occupants to cross with prams and pushchairs. Although it was a main line there was no control on this crossing and while the steam hauled trains ran quite regularly they were always fairly leisurely so there was little danger.

As kids we would often sit on the bridge and dare each other to drop small stones down the chimney of the engines as they passed underneath. Unfortunately there was usually too much smoke and steam so I do not remember anyone succeeding. Daft!

During the 50's one of the occupants kept a flock of geese in a large pen on the railway embankment at the eastern end of the houses. Up to the end of our period this little community was still under the auspices of British Rail. The area stayed virtually unchanged right up to the industrial development of modern times complete with the bad tempered horse who lingered on to the end of the swinging sixties. The same horse?

## Section Three – Portcreek

The above is the correct name but it more commonly known as Portscreek. Always a natural divider that kept Portsea Island isolated from the mainland it has altered considerably the last hundred years with the biggest upheaval taking place with the building of the A27 in the 1970s. Up to the period we are concerned with the changes had not been quite so drastic. Before any of todays bridges had been built it was a fairly well used channel for small craft and provided a direct route from Langstone Harbour through to Portsmouth harbour. Its high tide depth would have made it more than adequate for any of the vessels using it.

Where was the first crossing point? Probably around the site of the first bridge and the probability is that it was a ford only usable at low tide. This bridge was on a line from the Old Road directly across to the south shore of the creek. The biggest change prior to the building of the A27 was the blocking of a side channel which roughly followed the line of Highbury Grove in the area which is occupied by Cliffdale School. This left an island in midstream and the site of this was easily traceable in the mid 1950's. All of this area was mainly shingle. Although the bottom of the creek in the 50's was fairly deep in mud there were several areas where the base shingle still showed through. If we accept that this mud or silt is of comparatively recent origin then the probability of a ford being used as a crossing point in the distant past seems logical. One reason for the mud built up is the restriction on tidal flow caused by the bridges.

All of the north shore was low lying and prone to flooding until the creek wall was built by Mitchell's prior to the building of the Highbury Estate. The construction of the bank at the eastern end of the creek is described in the marshes section but that between the railway bridge and Portsbridge is somewhat different. It is far more sophisticated a typical period construction, built of rubble infill some six feet high and about twenty feet wide at its base. The side facing the water was vertical and faced with re-inforced concrete slabs and posts with topping blocks similar to oversized kerbstones. The top surface of this was wide enough to take an average sized lorry and consisted of compressed gravel between the railway and Chatsworth Avenue and crushed rubble from there to Tudor Crescent. From Pitreavie Road to Portsbridge it was a bit more primitive with just wooden stakes and a grass topping.

As well as being restrained with banks the natural tidal flow has had its movement interfered with by the hand of man on more than one occasion. The first of these restrictions was probably the first bridge. I have no idea of when it was or what it looked like. However, by the time we come to the 19th century it was probably a fairly substantial structure as it had to withstand stagecoaches which were the largest road vehicles of the day. Among the coaches used on the London run were the Royal Blue, the Independent, the Star of Brunswick and the Regular. A typical load was nine persons inside and up to eleven on top with the journey taking from nine to eleven hours. This bridge probably lasted well into the last half of the century when it was made obsolete by the new Portsbridge. This structure built in 1867 on the same site as the one that was there in the 1950's. With typical Victorian ingenuity and skill it was built as a sliding bridge with a hand winding mechanism that enabled the centre span of the bridge to telescope back to the island end. This was to enable the unrestricted passage of any shipping as was the railway bridge. This structure served for sixty years until it was replaced by the structure that most of us remember.

With the advent of WWII it was realised that with the Eastern Road bridge not yet completed it would only require one direct hit by a German bomb to render Britain's premier naval base completely isolated from the mainland. As a temporary measure (it lasted until the A27) was built) a structure always known as the Military Bridge (Peronne Road Bridge) was put up. It was basic in the extreme with a concrete pipe some five feet in diameter allowing the tide to flow through situated at low water level in mid stream and a solid infill laid over it from bank to bank. The sides sloped at about 45 degrees and were covered in concrete and a two lane road topped it off. It lasted with little or no maintenance for some thirty five years.

The railway bridge as such is described in the marshes section but beneath its centre span was a man-made island known to the locals in the 50's as the Cutfoot. It was around forty feet across and consisted of large granite blocks with shingle and mud holding them together. I do not know its purpose in life nor when it was built but it went with the road construction of the 70's as did the following item.

Either side of the bridge were groups of wooden posts in mid stream protruding out of the creek bed by about 12 – 15 feet. Their original purpose also remains obscure but local talk in the 50's linked them with wartime defences. If one looks at a photograph held by the City Records Office which shows the 1910 reconstruction of the railway bridge there are baulks of timber in the foreground of similar size. If they were used as part of the reconstruction work could they have lasted some sixty years in this environment?

During the 50's the creek became something akin to an open sewer with belts of scum containing all sorts of flotsam and jetsam, drowned puppies and kittens, raw sewerage etc.. Despite this sorry state, plenty of fish including some good sized bass were caught, bait was dug, and more to the point, children swam in it. At low tide the state was not a lot different and bore a strong resemblance to a rubbish tip. Bike frames, milk crates, corrugated iron, broken bottles and much, much more decorated the large expanse of black mud that was revealed. A small collection of boats were moored on the north eastern corner of the Military Bridge but to reach anything like open water in the form of Langstone Harbour the full length of the creek had to be traversed so not a lot of them saw much use.

The accompanying picture shows the telephone wires going across the railway bridge. In the early years of the 50's it was a common occurrence for swans, when flying low along the length of the creek to hit these wires and either fall into the water or, more seriously (especially for the swan) fall onto the railway lines. I never saw one killed but it often created mayhem for B.R. who would stop the trains and presumably cut off the power to the electric line. Fortunately the signal box was ideally sited to see the situation and the signalman, to his credit, always acted accordingly. Once the train had stopped it fell to the signalman, driver and guard to move the usually rather annoyed and puzzled bird back to the side of the signal box when the P.D.S.A. or the R.S.P.C.A would be called. If there was no obvious damage to the bird or it put up too much of a fight it was as gently as possible ushered over the side of the bridge into the water where, after a bit of preening, the swan regained its dignity and resumed its rudely interrupted journey.

Whether moved by human kindness or a concern for their timetables, B.R. had the telephone wires and poles taken down and the wires relaid at bridge level leaving the swans with an uninterrupted flight path.

In the 30's during construction of estate, Mitchells built a diving raft. I have been told that it was anchored towards the Portsbridge end of the creek. It had diving boards attached and was primarily for the use of the Highbury residents although I don't doubt that some of the work force found it useful. An advantage of swimming in the creek was that when the tide was out the sun warmed the mud and when the tide came in that warmth was transferred to the water – lovely!

The creek is now about half its original width and nowhere near as interesting. The one big improvement is the provision of a footbridge next to the railway bridge thus enabling anyone to visit the now more interesting south shore of the creek without having to walk about a mile to do so.

*Railway bridge looking east*

## Section Four – Between The Roads

This small area defies being given a title but because of its location has its own place in the development of the estate in that it is the focal point of two transport systems that would be used to bring the new residents to their equally new homes and would keep that standing for many years to come. The area is basically a triangle bounded by the railway, the Northern Road and the Portsmouth Road. Going back in time it was low lying land stretching in the direction of Portchester with only Little Wymering Farm showing any signs of usage. The first major use came with the building of the Portsmouth and Horndean Light Railway in 1903. Entering the area from the north over an iron bridge which crossed the main railway line about 20ft to the east of the present road bridge, it carried on south and joined the Portsmouth Corporation tram tracks almost opposite where the Portsbridge public house now stands. At this time the Corporation Tram Terminus was outside the block of shops still standing at the top of Windsor Road. The ground between this and the light railway was, at this time, used as a nursery and was therefore ideally sited for a developed tram terminus that came about. With the opening of the Northern Road in 1925 the area began to be tidied up and by the early 1930's some development

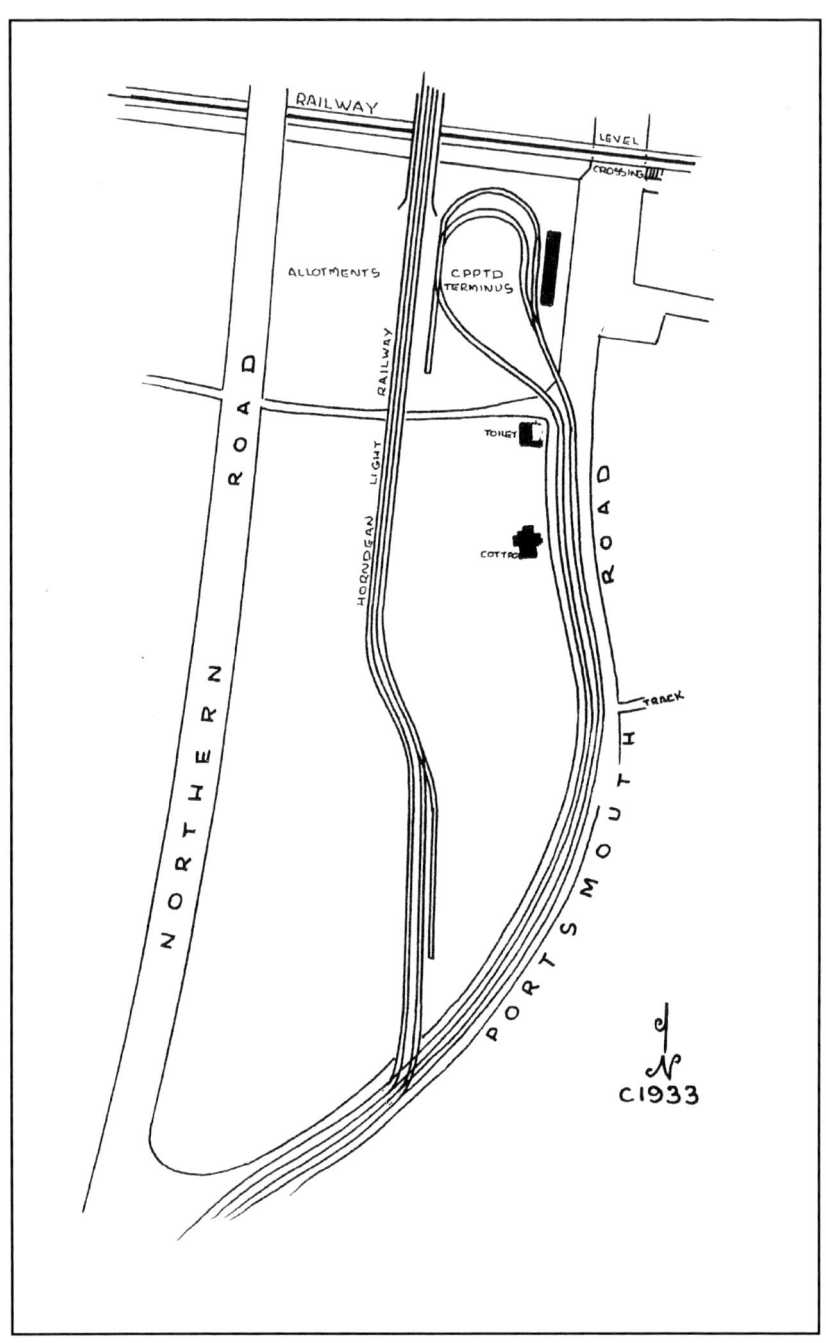

had begun. 1935 saw the end of the Horndean section and the subsequent lifting of the tracks. The Corporation terminus was much more long lasting feature and although changing from trams to trolleys to buses and shrinking a bit in the process is still holding fast. The old track that had once connected Little Wymering Farm to the Portsmouth Road served as a divider and eventually developed into the bus lane that connects the Northern and Portsmouth Roads. The small area bounded by these roads and the railway has, apart from the uses just mentioned, been used as allotments, the Collis Match factory in the 1950's and Roebuck House, with the latter causing the demolition of the old light railway bridge.

Going on to the area south of the bus lane probably the earliest buildings were two cottages opposite the entrance to Hawthorn Crescent. These survived to around the middle of the 1930's. On the corner of the bus lane and the Portsmouth Road were public toilets erected around 1930 and which lasted to around 1990 although closed for business for many of their final years. The old cottages mentioned had the joint name of Ivy Cottage. The Cosham Bowling Club opened around 1934 and used the old tramway booking office as its clubhouse. Further developments were another bowling green, tennis courts (grass and hard) and walkways with gardens. The fees for using the tennis courts were collected by the park keeper.

*Public Toilets*

Once these developments had taken place not much changed apart from S.E.B. having some sort of sub-station and a row of poplar trees growing along the route of the old light railway lines.

# Bowling

The original bowling club started around 1934 as the Cosham Bowling Club. It stayed as such until 1949 when a second green became available and six dissatisfied members broke away to form Highbury Bowling Club. This is as it is today with Cosham using the green nearest the Northern Road and Highbury using that nearest to the Portsmouth Road. The brick building is used by the Cosham Club and has been in existence since the early days whilst the wooden pavilion is home to both Highbury and to Cosham Ladies. This building is considerably older and started life as the ticket office for the Horndean Light Railway. It is at present a listed building but unfortunately could do with a bit of maintenance. This pavilion and green were at one time shared by Highbury and SESA (Southern Electricity) as their own bowling club. At one time the brick chalet had toilets which were open to the bowlers, players on the adjacent tennis courts and the general public. They were eventually bricked up from the outside and interior access was only laid on for the benefit of the bowlers.

Three clubs lease the facilities from the council as part of the Cosham Park Bowling Association with one representative from each of the Cosham, Highbury and Cosham Ladies Clubs (a ladies team have been in existence from the very beginning). The membership seems to have remained fairly constant over the years with about 50–60 in the Highbury Club.

Bowling seems to attract the 'older' person in general although it is definitely not an 'old persons' game and both the Highbury and Cosham clubs have produced some first class 'young' players over the years. The club members come from all walks of life and this makes for a friendly and interesting atmosphere. I have had many enjoyable times there and one incident in particular always comes to mind. Many years back one of our members was Cliff Parker, the ex -Pompey footballer. Although no longer playing the game, being 'in the know' he asked me if I would like any FA Cup Final tickets. Having no interest in the game, I said 'no'. However, when I returned home and casually mentioned this to father there was hell to pay as his interest in football was considerably greater than mine!

Highbury Club has its own distinctive badge in the form of a shield. It has a black background with gold edging and an intertwined HBC also in gold. Below the letters is a red Hampshire rose. At the time of writing the club was celebrating its 50th anniversary.

*Malcolm King*

## Northern Road

Opened in 1925 it was in reality a by-pass to take the increasing motor traffic away from the original road which consisted of the Portsmouth Road and Cosham High Street. The section which concerns us in this book contains nothing of note apart from an entrance to the bowling green area previously mentioned.

## Portsmouth Road

This was the original route into Portsmouth from Portsdown Hill through Cosham High Street and into what is now called the Old Road. The first Portsbridge on the present site was built in 1867 so around that time the Portsmouth Road veered onto its present course. The actual road runs from Cosham gates to Portsbridge.

By 1925 there were tea rooms run by the Misses Seymour at No 3, Mrs. Morris had a shop at No 7 and Mr. Locke had set up his tobacconist's shop at No 11. The shop was still known as Locke's well into the 50's but whether he was still the owner I do not know. This was followed by Windsor Terrace, a rather large building which in the 50's was externally much the same as when it was built. After that was Hawthorn Cottage. In the early 50's there was a cottage on the north corner of Hawthorn Crescent which was demolished to make way for the houses which at present occupy the site. In the first years of the 20th century a track was situated about half way between Hawthorn Crescent and Chatsworth Avenue which gave access to Little Salterns Cottage in Hawthorn Crescent. In about the same area a few years later there is mention of an entrance to Portsbridge Farm but whether it is the same track I do not know. I have spoken to a few people with pre-estate recollections who can vaguely recall what was possibly an old barn in that area which the builders of the estate later used to store materials in.

On the other side of the road immediately south of the railway was the Tramway and Light Railway Terminus. This was laid out in 1920 and still survives today albeit in a much reduced and far less interesting form. After this was the only building on the western side which consisted of a terrace of three houses. They had disappeared by 1934. By the same year commercial development had changed but not by much. No 5 was Miss White's School and No 7 had changed its proprietor to Mr. Cyril Pound. The tea rooms had gone but Mr. Locke was still going strong. The next building was the Portsbridge Hotel. The Portsbridge Hotel was built in the style of several other Portsmouth pubs in the 1930's and was to be the principal watering hole for the thirsty residents of the new estate. Externally it has changed very little over the years although the car park area has seen some alterations. The most noticeable has been the removal of the open fronted cubicles along the eastern boundary. These were complete with their own table and secluded bench seat beloved of many a young courting couple whispering sweet nothings over a glass of cider (11d a pint) or shandy (1/1d for the same amount). In the late 50's the establishment was complete with its own 'Guinness Queen' and several old gents who regularly played dominoes. Woe betide you if you happened to pinch one of their favourite seats .....!

The next building was the pumping station owned and operated by the Portsmouth Water Company. Built around 1930 it was a substantial brick structure occupying about one acre of ground. It never used to show any signs of activity but presumably had its uses a it lasted till 1996 when it was demolished.

On past the pumping station we come to the large grass area immediately prior to the creek. On this was a large 'birdcage' structure serving no purpose except to keep people away from a manhole cover which had been set on top of a mound three or four feet high. The cage was painted light green and had a twin on the other side of the creek. These manholes were access points to the large diameter water main of which the only purpose was to supply HM Dockyard. The cages were just extra security. They were erected in the 1920's and lasted till the motorway development during the 70's. At one stage during the 50's or 60's the cage on the south

*Portsmouth Water Company Boosting Station*

bank had roses growing over it. From memory a lot of children grew up thinking that they were cages for wild animals which for some reason never materialised. (They were cages for lions in my childhood – ed). Information supplied by Mr.. Bunyard.

By the mid 1950's the unused ground between Chatsworth Avenue and the Portsbridge public house had become earmarked for development of six private houses. They were numbered 65–75. The numbers 45–63 which, although not used, were originally allocated for premises between Hawthorn Crescent and Chatsworth Avenue. In the event the allocation was taken up by Highbury Buildings.

By 1956 the premises had changed again still not by a lot

No 1     Martin & Co., Electricians
No 3     Roberts, Funeral Directors
No 7     Butler & Cooke, Estate Agents
No 9     Smiths, Bakers

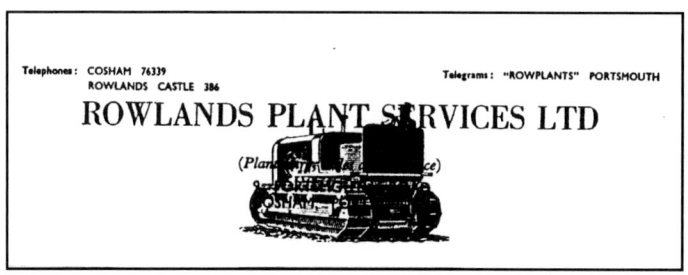

Telephones: COSHAM 76339
ROWLANDS CASTLE 386

Telegrams: "ROWPLANTS" PORTSMOUTH

**ROWLANDS PLANT SERVICES LTD**

(Plant Hire Service)

The rear of these premises was occupied by Rowlands Plant Hire. Formed in Rowlands Castle in the late 1940's the firm moved to Cosham soon after. They stayed in these premises until 1963 when a move was made to Northern Parade.

No 11    Hutchinson, Newsagent
No 13a   WVS Office
No 21    J Williams, Surveyor

## Highbury Buildings

Built in 1935 to tender to the needs of new residents of Highbury Estate it was then a modern style block of shops and homes. A good range of shops for 'everyday' needs with good quality accommodation above. Severely damaged by a bomb in the war it was rebuilt and still serves the community. In 1956 the premises were as follows:

No 1     N. Lazarus, Watchmaker
No 1a    Gilhams, Wool Stores

No 2     Williams, Fried Fish
         Very popular with the locals. As kids we always tried to make
         sure that we had 6d left at the weekend for a bag of chips. If we
         had an 1/– we could get a nice piece of cod to go with the chips.
         In those days it was all eaten out of sheets of newspaper. The
         shop was always closed on Mondays.
No 3     Willmontons, Greengrocers
No 4     Wilkes, Chemist
No 5     Carters, Sweetshop
         Another popular shop for the kids. I remember 1d chews, sherbert
         flying saucers made from rice paper, Sharpes rum toffees and
         many, many more.
No 6     Carters again. This time a greengrocers. Not so interesting.
No 7     Cracknell, Gents Outfitter. Good quality stuff.
No 8     Burtons, Butchers
No 9 & 10   Nappers, Ironmongers. An excellent selection of household
         paraphernalia was to be found here from screws to saucepans
         and nails to knobs.

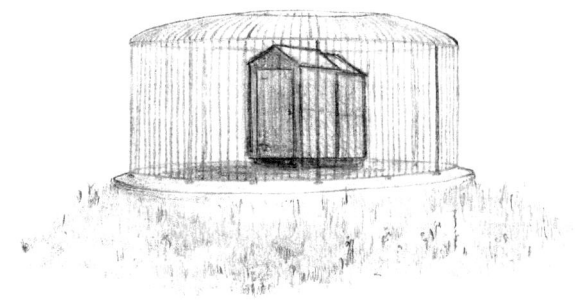

The above illustration is of the Water Company 'Cage' on the north
shore of the creek. It is shown with a small maintenance hut inside. This
was not a permanent feature.

## Section Five – Highbury Estate

## The Other Highbury

While visiting London in 1998 I found myself in the 'other' Highbury
in what is now the Borough of Islington. At the present time it is not very
different from any other part of the city or for that matter, any other large

conurbation. However, close your eyes for a minute and take yourself back some 200 years. You are in Highbury Fields situated on a hill with views in all directions across open country with the City of London some two miles to the south. Enterprising developers have decided that this spot would be superb housing that would outshine any other local development. The builders then get on with the erection of a Georgian style brick terrace which would be some of the best housing that money could buy. The finished building some 100 yards long with two breaks faced NW across a small park. This terrace became Highbury Place and facing it across the park was a shorter block although still four stories high which was named Highbury Terrace, a fact proclaimed in letters some two feet high carved in stone along its frontage with the date 1789 accompanying.

I cannot help but think that Mitchells had perhaps the same sort of outlook in mind when 'our' Highbury was being planned.

At the present time the view is still apparent but instead of fields all that is visible is high density Victorian and Edwardian buildings and modern development. Although I have said that the view is still there, you will have to find a gap between the buildings to actually see it!

## Highbury Estate

We now come to the major topic of this book, that of Highbury Estate itself. Started in the 'depression' years it must have seemed something akin to Utopia not only to those who were fortunate enough to live there but to those less so who could only look on the ultra modern housing and shops. Although to some extent self contained, it was within easy reach of Cosham shops or the 'downtown' shopping areas via the railway or a reliable bus service. An infants and juniors school was to be found on the estate itself whilst more equally modern schooling was available within a 20 minute walk.

Although grouped under the Highbury heading this is technically not correct. The heading in theory only covers Highbury, Chatsworth, Hawthorn and their adjoining roads when in fact, this section will cover some ten other roads. They have all been lumped together for convenience only.

Historically the area is full of just about nothing. The first building appears about one third of the way down what was to become Hawthorn Crescent on the railway side with a pond adjacent and was given the name of Little Salterns. Although this land was low lying I have no knowledge of it ever being regularly inundated by tidal action so the reason for the name is open to conjecture. Hawthorn Cottage was on the corner of the crescent with the Red House and Portsbridge Cottages along the Old Road seem to complete the buildings of the 19th century although there is some possibility of farm buildings scattered around the area. The area immediately neighbouring the railway station is also older than the main estate but this will be dealt with alphabetically.

The original road onto Portsea Island took approximately the line of the Old Road and at its junction with the creek was to be found a fort. This was the island's first line of defence against any insurgent threat from the mainland and was built in 1643. In 'Portsmouth that has Passed' by W. G. Gates it is shown as what appears to be an earthen bank through which the road passes under an arch. There appear to be two storey buildings just inside the bank. Just to the north the village of Cosham was growing but the area between the railway and the creek was left virtually untouched until the mid 1920's.

At about this period the population was expanding and throughout the country new estates and even new towns were being built. Local authorities had also realised that some of the older housing was not just old but way below standard and the only way to sort it out was not to try to modernise but to pull it down and rebuild. Highbury was to meet the call for a better class of housing that was needed for the ever expanding 'middle class' of the working population and was thus an innovation in its own right. On the developers publicity map, Highbury Estate not only encloses its present area but about half of East Cosham marches, the area north of the railway between Court Lane and Salisbury Road and even further north onto the hill slopes between East Cosham Road, St. Martins Road and London Road, i.e. the Courtmount Grove area. What date this was drawn up and if indeed, it was a misprint, I do not know but seeing as it was all carefully shaded I think that perhaps this was an intended development which for one or maybe several reasons, shrunk during the incubation period. As we all know, it did not work out like that which fortunately makes my job a lot easier. It is also interesting to note that the original plan did NOT cover any development between Highbury Grove and the creek. This leads me to the assumption that the area was either already earmarked for development by A. N. Other or what seems to be more likely, already under construction.

Up to the end of our period (around 1960) the estate developed in two basic phases separated by the war. Pre-war saw the 'Highbury Houses' and post-war saw the unfinished portion – something less than one quarter of the area, given over to prefabs. These were pulled down in the early 60's and replaced with flats and maisonettes.

The area between Highbury Grove and the creek in the SW corner of the estate was and sometimes still is known as the 'Dockyard Estate' and was built to house key members of HM Dockyard, Rosyth in Scotland, where large numbers of men had been made redundant in the 20's. Apparently started just prior to the Highbury area there was no direct connection between the two. Some of the road names tie in with Scotland, i.e. Pitreavie, Elgin and Donaldson but others don't seem to. Any information on this would be gratefully received.

On the 22nd of August 1930, aged 14 years, a 'Stamshaw Chicken' and proud of it, I left my home in Jervis Road and walked northwards along a lane with open fields on either side towards Hilsea. The only buildings were around Hilsea Crescent and that lane was to become Northern Parade. It was then on across Portsbridge and into the Portsmouth Road at Cosham and what was to become my workplace for the next nine years.

I was on my way to become an apprentice painter and decorator to Mitchell & Sons, the builders who had got the contract to construct the Highbury Estate. My first sight of the works were the workshops and offices which were corrugated iron buildings and stood on the site later to be occupied by Highbury Buildings.

The emphasis on this new estate was that it was to be 'craftsmen built' and this was very true. My apprenticeship was to be five years duration with evening classes all paid for by my employers. My wages were to start at 7/6d per week (37.5p). Bricklayers and plasterers got 10/–. My money would increase by £1 per year and at the end of five years I would get my indentures. It was a good place to learn a trade as all of the craftsmen could be relied on to teach you as you went along, the more you asked, the more you learnt. They were all proud of their individual trades and looked the part, all had their tools which they looked after, cleaned at the end of the day and put in their bags or boxes. Their wages were fairly good for that period and ranged from £5 – £8 per week.

As time passed and I got settled into this way of life, I got myself a pushbike. It was a Hercules with drop handlebars. To make life a bit easier and to safeguard my new possession I changed my route to work by using London Road as it had a metalled surface which made pedalling a lot easier.

The apprentices were involved in all aspects of the work but according custom were given the inside of cupboards to practice on. As I already knew something about signwriting I was put to work on a large advertising hoarding. As well as just advertising the houses it had a wooden cut out of a terrace superimposed on it all of which had to be painted properly. When it was finished it was erected alongside the railway line. One good thing about working on the sign was that I was working away from the main works and there was a good deal more freedom to skylark and get away with it. Although it was a good organisation to work for, rules were rules and if you got caught mucking about you were punished. This usually meant being given all the grotty jobs on the site until the foreman considered that you had done your bit. Fortunately most of us took this in good humour and there were seldom any ill feelings.

When I started the whole area was just open fields with the bank along Portcreek being built up to keep the water at bay. The area grew with Highbury being built first, followed by Chatsworth and Hawthorn. All the wooden structures for the houses were made on site, roof trusses, window frames and stairs etc. all of these coated in pink primer before being taken to be installed after which they were given two coats of undercoat and then gloss. The potential buyer could have the choice of colour or if he wished, the wood could be grained to represent a variety of woods – maple, teak, etc.

As far as we knew , the roads were named after well known country houses to give the impression of luxury homes – which indeed they were. There were three types and the original prices were £640 for an end of terrace which included a garage, £540 for the one next to it which had a bay window to the front bedroom and £525 for the inner ones in the terrace.

Mitchell's were a very forward thinking firm for the time and built a social club on the site for the use of the workforce and their families and also for the new residents because a site of this size obviously took a long time to build and in fact had not been completed by the outbreak of war. The clubhouse in Dovercourt Road was a typical period design and lasted into the late 50's as Highbury Infants School.

As the houses progressed down the roads the workshops were moved to the Portcreek end of Dovercourt Road. These huts lasted until long after the war and were finally demolished with the building of the A27. During the late 40's and 50's they were used by Lucas', the yacht chandlers. The space left when the original workshops moved to this location was taken up with Highbury Buildings.

One further thing I will add is that Mitchells' only had dealings with the roads I have mentioned. Pitreavie, Tudor, Donaldson, Jasmond, Elgin, Edgerly and I believe the Old Road were known as the 'Naval Estate' (There is some evidence that Dockyard personnel came from Pembroke Dock and Milford Haven areas in South Wales as well as Scotland) and were built by what we called the 'Dockyard Mateys'. Despite this, the houses had a lot in common with each other but whether this was by accident or design I do not know.

I can look back on those times with pleasure and pride and feel sure that both the original and subsequent owners will have suffered very little in the way of major problems with their property.

*William Stacey*

22

We will now progress on a road by road basis in alphabetical order. As the estate is not too large or complex any commercial usage will be given for both 1934 and 1956. Any house numbers that are not mentioned were residential only. The information has been put together using the Kelly's street directories for the years listed.

## Chatsworth Avenue

Chatsworth House in Derbyshire was built between the years 1687 and 1706 as the home of the Duke of Devonshire. It is classed as one of the country's classic homes and this was presumably the impression that the estates developers wished to convey to prospective purchasers. The story by William Stacey seems to confirm this. Although apparently not the first road to be built, in the 1929/30 directory it contained only one of Mitchell's homes to be occupied in that year, number 14.

*South Side*

| | |
|---|---|
| 4 | 1956 F. Penney, Dentist |
| 60 | 1956 N.S.P.C.C. Inspectors Office |
| 82 | 1956 Drs. Martingale, Thompson & Brown, Doctors Surgery. |

"I remember Dr. Brown very well. It was him to whom my mother rushed me when I had an accident on my pushbike. I had hit the back of a stationary lorry and got a deep cut on my cheek which warranted three stitches. Aged about 14 I was quite proud of this 'major' wound – a pride that disappeared very quickly about five days later when he took the stitches out. Their removal hurt a lot more than their insertion!"

All three doctors were popular with their patients.

84　　　In 1934 was a grocery shop and post office run by Mr. Eggerton. By 1956 and to the end of our period the grocery side had gone to be replaced by a newsagents but the Post Office side stayed on to be run by Mr. Purnell.

"The shop was well stacked with all sorts of bits and pieces and for some reason I remember that it was a lot darker at the newsagents area than at the Post Office end."

86　　　Was always the Co-op, grocers.

"Mum would always buy her cigarettes there. I got her to smoke Turf as there were always cards to collect inside. This was in the days before cellophane wrapping and the girl behind the till would let me go through the packets until I found a card that I needed. The aeroplane set were always my favourites."

Next door to the Co-op lived one of the girls who used to be in our crowd and we would regularly go to call for her. The conversation was always the same. 'Good afternoon Mrs. Madin, is Viv coming out?' 'My daughter was christened Vivienne.' Door shuts. Repeat the performance but changed to 'Is Vivienne coming out?' One of those totally unimportant things that stay in your memory over the years.

134      1934 Highbury School for Girls and Prep School for Boys. The principal was Mrs. D. Lawrence.

192      1956 Mrs. Border, Greengrocer.

*North Side*

1a      1956 Staplefords' Funeral Directors, office

5      1934 King & King, Estate Agents, office

75      Carrolls General Store.
Was there right from the beginning of the estate and stayed as such 'till the end of our period when it continued in the same line of business for a few more years under the name of Mead.

77      Harfields, Hairdressers
Was a father and son team and has been there since the early days of the estate. In later years it was run solely by the son, Harry, who had a passion for Jaguars as his means of transport. "He had a board that he would put on the arms of the adults chair to seat children. Eventually you would be allowed to sit in the chair. You then knew that you had grown up. Under the wash basins there was a slanting trap door that he would lift up and sweep all the hair cuttings into. I always wondered where it went to but never got around to asking. In the 50's Harry knew most of the kids by name and probably most of the adults as well. I think there was a Ladies Hairdresser upstairs but I am not sure."

79      In 1956 this was Dr. Nichols (Mrs.), Surgery. I don't think it lasted much past this date. However, it had been a surgery for many years as in 1934 Dr. Reeves was there.

133      1934 Miss Cobhan, Music Teacher

187      1934 At this time this number was the last in the road and was occupied by Whites', Confectioners.

189      Lush & Co, Off Licence

In the 1950's from Wembley Grove to the end of the avenue the road surface changed from a pinkish coloured concrete to nothing better than a farm track. Strictly speaking this did not go to the very end but for some reason the last section in front of two Council prefabs was surfaced in Tarmac.

## Donaldson Road

This road forms part of the Naval Estate and is residential. The road originally had direct access to the Portsmouth Road but this was blocked off with the building of the new roundabout and flyover in the 70's. A Doctor Donaldson was an instigator in getting Cathedral status for St. Thomas in the High Street, Old Portsmouth, but I can find no definite connection.

## Dovercourt Road

Just possibly named after the Mansion called 'Cliff House' in Dovercourt, in Essex built by a John Bagshaw M.P. for Harwich in 1847. He also bought land at Lower Dovercourt for a 'new town'. His mansion was demolished in 1909.

Basically a joining road it was residential from its junction with Highbury Grove southwards. At the end of the houses it became a rough track. This led to the creek bank to the workshop area of the estate builders when they moved from the Cosham end to keep pace with the building progress. On the eastern side immediately after the houses was the entrance to Vosper's playing field. This was a large area now occupied by Highbury College. In the 50's it had two football pitches and a cricket pitch surrounded by rough ground. It saw very little use by its owners but was a Mecca for the Estates' children. There was a small, green, wooden pavilion near the entrance with a verandah which provided cover for the kids when it was raining. Next to this was a hut which I never knew to be opened but which I assume was used to house the groundsman's equipment. Between the two was a large and very rusty petrol driven lawnmower.

I remember that the field would often freeze during wet weather and sometimes, if it was cold enough, it would freeze over and provide a good skating rink. Most of the time we used it to play football or cricket. A local used to tether her horse there. I think its name was 'Flicker'.

On the west side of the road was another typical thirties style pavilion. Originally put up by the estate builders as a club for the new residents of the estate. It was also open to the workforce employed on the still growing development of Highbury. It appears that the onset of war stopped it from really getting going and during the war it was taken over by the local electricity board and used by them as a sports and social club for their employees. It was also used to stage social functions for troops stationed in the area. After the war it reverted to members only and became a successful club with a dance floor, billiards and a small bar. The area behind the club was an enclosed sports field. The fact that it was enclosed enabled it to host Hampshire league football matches and also some of the early F.A. Amateur Cup games. Summer saw the same enthusiasm applied to cricket.

By the early 50's the need for a local school had become apparent. In the original estate development plan a school had been catered for but, like so many other things, the war put a stop to it. Highbury Primary School was officially opened by Councillor Blake on 2nd March 1954 although the present building did not take its first intake of pupils until 2nd December that year. It started off with 283 children although with the accommodation being a bit cramped, one class used the staff room and two of the infants' classes used St. Phillips Church Hall. The wooden club building survived for a short time after this and was used for infant classes until its demolition. Prior to the official opening all the infant classes seem to have been split between the old club building and St. Phillips.

The original staff were as follows:

The Headmaster was Mr. Law, who was ably assisted by Mr. Frazier, Mr. Caddy, Mr. Goble, Mr. Burrows, Mrs. Martin, Miss Worley, Miss Bennett, Mrs. Carter, Mrs. Godfrey and Mrs. Jackson.

The school settled into the pattern of the period with its own school uniform – grey jacket and skirt (or trousers) with a cap for the boys and a beret with a tassel for the girls. The school blouses were Mayflower – red, Victory – green, Revenge – blue, and Vanguard – yellow.

Sportsday was an annual occasion with all the usual events plus one that I have never heard of – 'The Late for School' competition and yes, you could even get a certificate for it!

The school appeared to teach 'double writing' in the 'Marion Richardson' style (She was a London Schools inspector and introduced the style in 1935 – Ed). This was peculiar in the respect that the letters did not have loops, just straight lines. This style was also taught at Court Lane around the same period.

I went to Court Lane at the age of ten having just learnt double writing with loops at Solent Road. I then was told to stop using loops and do it the 'Marion Richardson' way, i.e. no loops. After one year I passed the eleven plus and went to Portsmouth Technical School – "use loops boy, you're not a baby now!" (Same experience Lyndhurst Road Juniors to Northern Grammar, ten years later – Ed)

"In 1954 I lived at number 281 Hawthorn Crescent which was a 'prefab'. I was 10 years old . My sister, Moira, was also an original pupil but was two years younger than me. I had started my education in St. Phillips Church Hall and also spent some time in the Electricity Club which was also used as a school. The club occupied a site close to where the present school now stands. The year before the present school opened I was attending Court Lane School.

When the one in Dovercourt Road opened, all the children of the estate who were of the appropriate age had to attend the new school. The exception were those who were to take their eleven plus during the coming year. It was thought that a change of school might adversely affect their chances of success. Those children were given the option of moving to the new school or not. My parents left the decision to me and consequently I became one of the original pupils. There were very few of us aged ten and we must have been a pretty dim lot! Any child likely to pass the eleven plus would have probably done better to have stayed at his or her original school.

The new school was lovely. Court Lane had been very crowded with large classes. If my memory serves me right, there were only sixteen of us in our class. Our teacher was Mr. Caddy and I came to have a strong affection for him. The headmaster was Mr. Law; he had come from Flying Bull Lane school. That was a tough school and he was a formidable man. I remember him as being keen on sport and recall his enthusiasm for soccer, cricket and athletics, all of which I took part in during my year at the school.

Mr. Caddy was an excellent teacher who spent a lot of his time with me and another boy named Derrick Skinner who was brighter than I was. I made a great deal of progress while in his class and particularly remember the coaching he gave us doing the old eleven plus exam papers. I was not a well behaved boy but I think I was liked for my naughtiness. I remember Mr. Caddy paying me 2/6d (12/5p) if I would agree to be well behaved when a student teacher was to have the class for a fortnight.

I will always remember the school sports day in the early summer of 1955. I had done quite well, winning the sprint and the long jump. My mother was very pleased at my sporting prowess but her great joy was to be told that I had passed my eleven plus to go to the Northern Grammar School."

*Dr. Adrian Riley*

At its southern end the road went into the premises of Lucas & Son, Sailmakers. The buildings had been put up before the war when the estate was still being built. They were right up against the creek bank and consisted of (I believe) one long hut and some smaller outbuildings. At one stage in the mid 50's the surrounding yard housed a complete and fairly large yacht which was lifted out by a large crane on the creek bank and deposited in the creek at high water. Why, I never found out. It could not have sailed out as there were bridges at either end so I assume it was lifted out again and taken away by road although I have no recollection of ever seeing a vehicle of the required size on the roads of the estate.

The mystery is solved in the following story:

"At its southern end the road went into a small jumble of huts, large and small. These started life as the joinery workshops and stable of Mitchell's, the estate's builders. The stables were needed owing to the considerable quantity of horses which at that time were still in use for large building projects such as Highbury. A little known fact was that Mitchell also kept pigs there.

Post War, the Council were the owners of the area and rented it to Lucas', the chandlers, who had been bombed out of their Old Portsmouth premises. Other people who were also looking for small premises in which to ply their trade came to these buildings among whom were Mr. Perry and Mr. Feltham – both well known in the boating fraternity. The former started to pursue his hobby in about 1935 by making sail battens and headboards for Lucas' until 1959 when he went full time. Lucas' eventually moved out but Mr. Perry stayed on until 1967 when the Education Department of the Council wanted their land. During those eight years some 20 boats were built, mainly yachts of 20–33 feet in length and of wooden construction. However, towards the end, a few launches were built and fibreglass was beginning to make its presence felt.

When the boats were finished, the normal practice was to hire a large crane and position it on the creek towpath, lift the yacht out of the yard and into the creek – high tide was an obvious must. It was then floated into Langstone Harbour. To achieve this, the mast would be lowered and with a careful study of the tidal conditions, the boat could be passed under both bridges into the open water beyond.

Tudor Sailing Club, which spent most of its life in its Eastern Road premises, started off here after the war under the driving force of Mr. Madins whose home was in Chatsworth Avenue. The club moved to its premises on the Eastern Road immediately adjacent to the SE end of the water bridge around 1949."

The preceding information was gratefully received from Mr. John Perry.

**Edgerley Gardens**, possibly named after a small village in Shropshire. Residential only

| | |
|---|---|
| 15 | Mrs. Gemmell, a maternity nurse was here in 1934 but by 1956 she had moved to Hawthorn Crescent. |
| 23 | Mr. Newbold, music teacher |

"A friend of mine, doing his paper round, decided that it would save a lot of time if, instead of going back down the path and into the next house via the gate, he just vaulted the fence. The fences, a lot of which still exist, were a thin concrete grid cast around a metal reinforcing wire and were purely ornamental, nothing more. They were certainly not designed for vaulting he lost his paper round."

## Elgin Road
Named after the cathedral town in Scotland. A double ended cul-de-sac. Residential only.

## Hawthorn Crescent
Probably named after Hawthorn Cottage which stood on the NE corner of its junction with Portsmouth Road. There was a cottage there until the mid 50's but whether it was the original or not I do not know. From what little that I can remember of it I think it to be unlikely. This appears to have been the last of the three major roads on the estate to have been built.

*North Side*

| | |
|---|---|
| 91 | 1956 saw it occupied by Jane Gemmill, midwife. This was presumably the same lady who lived in Edgerley Gardens before the war. |
| 123 | On the 1870 map this is around the area known as Little Salterns. By 1934 there was small cottage known as Portsbridge Cottage. This is a bit confusing as the same name is applied to cottages in the Old Road. In the 1950's it was a small whitish or cement rendered building with orchard occupying the ground now used by Nos. 125–137. The only occupant I recall was an old lady. "In the early 50's we would leave Court Lane School for our dinner break and if we ran we would be in time to see the 12.10 'Streak'. This was the Brighton to Cardiff (or Exeter?) Express train and was always hauled by a West Country or Battle of Britain class steam locomotive. The best view was to be obtained from the alley that ran along the backs of the houses in Hawthorn Crescent. We inevitably ran through the cottage garden (there were no gates and the fence was down) and if the old lady saw us we would either be told off or alternatively offered a bag of apples from the orchard." |

The cottage was demolished in the mid 50's and Nos. 125–137 were built on the site. Interestingly those numbers were omitted in the original numbering system which appears to point to the possibility that the person owning that piece of land would not sell it to the developers when the estate was being built.

In the 1934 listing the last house was No 195, on the north side of the road.

267      St. Phillips Church and Vicarage.

One of the few downsides to the estate was that the nearest parish church was about a mile distant. In 1934 the Bishop of Portsmouth received an offer of £25,000 from Lady Mary Harrison for the purpose of providing a church, a hall and a vicarage in the developing area. The area chosen was Highbury and Sir Ninian Comper, one of the country's leading ecclesiastical architects, was chosen to design it. Although the outside is a period design, the interior is a different matter and to quote Sir John Betjeman, 'You would never know from the outside how breathtaking is the interior'.

Comper's son, Sebastian, designed the hall and vicarage and these were the first to be completed in 1936. The church itself was built by Frank J. Privett Ltd., and was completed the following year.

In the mid 50's the church hall was home to two youth groups, St. Phillips Boys Club which met on Saturdays between 6 and 9pm and the Young Communicants Guild on Wednesdays between 6.45 and 9.45pm. The former groups' leader was Mr. Porteous and the activities centred around football, cricket, indoor games, discussions and play reading etc., whilst the latter had the Rev K. King as a leader with their time taken up with talks, discussions, dancing and games. I think the two groups amalgamated by the end of the decade to form a club catering for all of these activities for both sexes.

"The church hall was often used by the estate residents for various events. In the late 50's a youth club was well established but as it was mainly for churchgoers there was some conflict between those who ran the club and those who wanted to join but did not attend church. However, after one or two low key arguments the problem seemed to blow over and everybody was made welcome. The entertainments were darts, table tennis and dancing to rock music from a record player. The usual scene was the boys played darts, both sexes played table tennis and the girls danced (usually with each other). Any of the boys not engaged in an activity would usually sit around the edges of the hall just watching the dancing and occasionally taking the mickey.

Outside near the railway was a small corrugated iron toilet block the roof of which made a splendid vantage point for the train spotters of which there were a good many on the estate."

"My first months at school were spent in St. Phillips Church Hall in

Hawthorn Crescent whilst the development of the school in Dovercourt Road was completed. There were two classes held in the hall and were separated by a large curtain. My first teacher was Miss Walsh, who I still remember with fear and trepidation. She ruled her classes with a rod of iron, but I have to admit that she taught me to read and to spell well, something for which I have had cause to thank her for many times in my life."

*Mrs. Evelyn Grant*

Next to the church was the local Scout hut.

"Highbury's own group of cubs and scouts was formed in 1937 and was registered as the 32nd Portsmouth (Highbury). It is possible that the Brownies and Guides were formed at the same time. They used St. Phillips Church Hall as a meeting place but unfortunately, after a short time, there was a disagreement with the Vicar and they moved to a garage like building vacated by Mitchell's, the estate developers. Eventually, in 1939, another scout group was formed by the church which met in the hall with the new designation of the 62nd Portsmouth (St. Phillips).

The group met in the church hall until 1959/60 when they acquired their own headquarters. This was one of the American WWII wooden huts erected in the ground of the Portsmouth Technical School and used as a school music room. In 1958 the proposed school development saw no future for the huts. This particular one was saved and brought to the Hawthorn Crescent site where it was officially opened by the Hampshire Scout County Commissioner, Air Vice Marshall C. N. H. Bilney.

The group catered for 18–24 boys in the cub pack and a similar number in the scouts troop. The cubs held pack holidays at Fernhurst, Sway and Brockenhurst in the New Forest and at Langton Maltravers near Swanage while the scouts enjoyed camping in the Heyshott, Dockenfield and Hursley areas. The HQ of the Paulsgrove Scouts in Carlton Road was often used as a base for exercises on Portsdown Hill.

The journey to camp was an adventure. For short journeys, reliance was placed on parents to help with transport but for trips further a field, a removal van provided by councillor Ashley or a coach hired from Meatyards of Portchester were used. When using the van everyone piled in the back sitting on tents and equipment. With the coach we could get three cubs to a pair of seats, the boxes of food on the back seats and the tents and poles in the aisle. With today's safety regulations these informal and enjoyable ways of transporting young children would be somewhat frowned upon. During this period it was the norm to have a family day during camp week. The whole family could and would come down to visit. Sometimes this would result in one or two lads getting homesick and going back home with mum and dad. A greater problem were the food parcels that worried parents brought to supplement camp food. This food was usually consumed at an unofficial midnight binge with the resulting lack of appetite the next day. Fortunately the visiting practice faded into oblivion.

The groups' cubs and scouts always did well in the scout swimming competitions and the cubs were frequent winners of the city colour competition. This was for a flag presented by the Portsmouth Evening News to promote friendly rivalry between the then four Portsmouth scout districts."

*Mr. & Mrs. Spiller.*

Any development that had been in the plans for the southeast end of the crescent was halted by the war and with the post war demand for housing, something that could be erected a lot quicker than conventional housing was required. This was met by the delivery of 100 single storey prefabricated homes supplied by the USA under the Lease-Lend Agreement set up during the war. Manpower was supplied by men being released from the forces and being used under contract to the Ministry of Works. The ease and speed of erection was shown by reports that after eight weeks, 80% of the prefabs (as they became known) were complete. They were of a different type to most others in the city and were made up of what I have been told was millboard. This was a soft fibrous board built into wooden frames. They contained two bedrooms of a reasonable size with a living room, kitchen, bathroom and W.C., an airing cupboard and an entrance hall. Heating and hot water were supplied by a very efficient coal fire with a back boiler connected to a tall, thin storage tank in the kitchen. The kitchen had fitted cupboards and a built in larder but unlike most others in the city did not have a fridge. They had fair size gardens back and front with small sheds made from redundant Anderson Shelters.

They started next to St. Phillips Church and on the railway side were arranged conventionally one deep to the far end of the road. On the other side of the road the layout was less conventional. A path led towards the backs of the houses in Chatsworth Avenue. At the end of this path was one prefab. On the right of it were two others. This pattern was repeated to the end of the road. Although usually referred to as the Hawthorn Crescent Prefab Estate there were five more at the end of Highbury Grove and a further three at the bottom of Chatsworth Avenue. They were warm, dry and comfortable and although originally only meant to stay in use for about five years they served the council for more than double that time, finally being demolished around 1961 to make way for the flats and maisonettes that now grace the area.

At the far end of the road was a timber yard but whether it was in Hawthorn Crescent or Highbury Grove I do not know nor do I know its name. It went up as far as the creek bank and up to the railway fence. It consisted of two Nissen huts and a variety of other sheds. Between it and the last houses in Highbury Grove and bounded north by Highbury Grove and the south by the creek, was a fair sized patch of rough ground. At one stage in the 50's someone erected a very large Nissen hut on it but for what purpose was never revealed. To my knowledge it served but two purposes:– one for the local kids to play and shelter and the other as a nesting site for a swallow. It lasted until the new A27 was built. The field itself was an ideal play area and was the traditional spot for the November 5th bonfire.

## Highbury Grove

"Our family moved into No 349 during the school summer holidays in 1952. Our new home was a prefab made of what I was later told was millboard although I still do not know if this was the correct name. Small but warm and comfortable with HOT RUNNING water! An Anderson shelter served as the garden shed although Dad had brought his own much bigger one with him from our previous home so we finished up with two. It was an ideal area for a ten year old boy with plenty of rough ground and bushes on which to build dens, light fires and play Cowboys and Indians. My new found friends and I used the creek as a swimming pool and several of us learnt to swim in it. Looking back, what with the currents, deep water and mud it was probably quite dangerous but like all kids we didn't see any danger even when it was pointed out to us and we never took any notice. On top of this was the accumulated filth that came in and out with many of the tides. Every time we got a cold we thought we had developed polio which was fairly rife at the time but fortunately none of us ever did.

East Cosham marshes provided a much bigger adventure area but was only accessible if the tide was low and we could get under the railway bridge. High tide meant a long detour through the Railway Triangle. The new friends that I made were into train spotting and I soon joined the craze and developed a love of steam trains that remains with me to this day. We would buy a season ticket during the summer holidays at a cost of 5/– rising to 7/6d after a couple of years. This provided us with unlimited travel over a certain area for one week. Our favourite haunts were Eastleigh and Southampton Central where we could see the 'glamour' trains like the Bournemouth Belle and the Cunarder. In those days you could travel on your own at a tender age with no worries at all. Train spotting then did not carry the 'mockable' image that it seems to carry today and, as far as I know, anoraks were not available.

In 1953 Dad decorated the front of the prefab with flags of the Commonwealth to celebrate the Coronation and there was a big community party on the waste ground behind the prefabs alongside the church about where the present community centre now stands. We had food set out on tables, races and games. There was a plastic carrier bag with souvenirs for the children and a red, white and blue baseball cap (1953 version) for the grown ups which apart from not fitting made their heads sweat profusely.

I made a lot of good and long lasting friendships in the four years that we lived there and researching this book found me rediscovering a lot of old names that had been forgotten over the years."

*Author*

**Highbury Grove**, the 'flagship' road of the estate. No proof to date of the origin of the name. There is a small village of this name in Somerset and an area in London complete with its own football stadium but I see no connection apart from what I have written at the very beginning of the Highbury section. A wider road than others with grass verges and trees. Residential with few exceptions.

*North Side*

| | |
|---|---|
| 89 | This was the original show house |
| 119 | Miss Bickford, Accountant |
| 121 | Mr. Wallen, Insurance Agent |

*South Side*

| | |
|---|---|
| 96 | Hugh Sells, Physician & Surgeon |

This was how the road stood in 1934, finishing at nos 187 and 174 respectively. By 1956 even these small ventures into the commercial world had disappeared. However, in the mid 50's the last terrace and bungalows were built on the waste ground on the south side of the road with the last building of these being a small shop.

"Prior to these being built this was just open ground between the road and the creek bank. In among the bushes etc. were some foundations made of brick forming two rectangles roughly the size of wartime army huts. Their use has always eluded me until very recently when I heard a story that during the war there was an anti-aircraft battery there."

Reverting to the shop, it was a small general store and was run by a Mr. and Mrs. Pascoe. Mrs. Pascoe would make large numbers of ice lollies during the hot weather which she would sell for the princely sum of 1d each. The author's mother was the shop's first customer and we have the photograph taken at the time. On the other side of the road were five prefabs Nos 345–353.

In recent times a local builder recalled an incident concerning some lintels over the windows in some of the pre-war houses. The story goes that at the time of building, some of the old tramlines in the Cosham area were being taken up and the builders bought up a lot of them, cut them to suitable lengths and used them as lintels! True or not? I don't know but it makes a good tale.

## Highbury Way

This was originally part of Highbury Grove. There were no buildings, only the entrance to Portsmouth Trading Co. whose address was actually listed in the Old Road. When PTC ceased trading here the area was quickly snapped up for housing. Rather than give addresses such as A1, B1 Highbury Grove or similar, this short length of road was given its present name around 1961.

## Jasmond Road

Possibly named after one of the developers, residential.

## (The) Old Road

This was actually the course of the old route into Portsmouth until the present system came into being. Until the estate was built it appeared to have but three residents listed in 1925 as Mr. James Woodsford in the Red House and John Taylor in Portsbridge Cottage, the third resident was in Portsbridge Farm. At the Tudor Crescent end lay Portsbridge Farm. The cottage and the farm have long since disappeared but the Red House still survives at the junction with Highbury Way. The cottage stood approximately where nos 6–16 now stand and the site was originally earmarked for the new Highbury Tennis Club which apparently never materialised. In between its demise and the building of the present houses the area was used as allotments. The cottage was listed until 1934.

On the west side where PTC was based in later years, the first occupants were Mitchells' the estate builders. No 19 housed Mrs. Granville, a teacher of music. Perhaps the property that springs to most peoples' minds in this road was the shop run by Mr. Kitchen in the Red House who dealt with cycles and radios right up to his demise in fairly recent years.

Immediately following is an excellent factual and first hand account of Mr. Kitchen and his business but like so many books dealing with history, information from one source can often clash with that from another. It does however, make for interesting reading so in the interests of impartiality I will give the statement that is contrary to the information in the story. This states that the Red House was completed but that the southern end was pulled down by Mitchell's to allow for the building of Highbury Grove (Way). What cannot be disputed is that when the building was first built there would have been uninterrupted views from it right along the northern reaches of Portsea Island and beyond.

"The Red House – Apparently the building first came on the scene around the middle of the 19th century as a Customs and Excise House on the Old Portsmouth Road. It is believed that it was originally going to be twice the present size but was never completed. It presumably went into private ownership and in later years became the property of Mr. Mitchell who was responsible for the development of most of Highbury Estate.

In the late 1930's Mr. Les Kitchen and his father transferred their business from Eastney to the Red House which they rented from Mr. Mitchell. At this time Les Kitchen and his wife were already living on the estate. In 1958 however, they transferred their residency to the Red House. Les Kitchen took over the business in 1954 and in the same year purchased the building from Mr. Mitchell. Les was a bit of a character and a keen sea fisherman as well as being a passionate billiards and snooker player who was still playing his favourite game right up to his death in 1991.

The business started with the making and repairing of radios from which trade came the name of the shop – Radio Mart. In the early post war years government surplus was sold and this continued until about 1954 when all the old stock was disposed of. Trading then took on a new front with the sale of televisions, radios and all household electrical appliances. He also established his own TV rental business which continued until colour TV came on the scene.

Around 1969 he changed again, this time the cycle trade being his mainstay. One thing that could be guaranteed to upset Les concerned people who would buy a cycle through the medium of a catalogue. This would invariably tell the proud purchaser to 'take your new cycle along to your

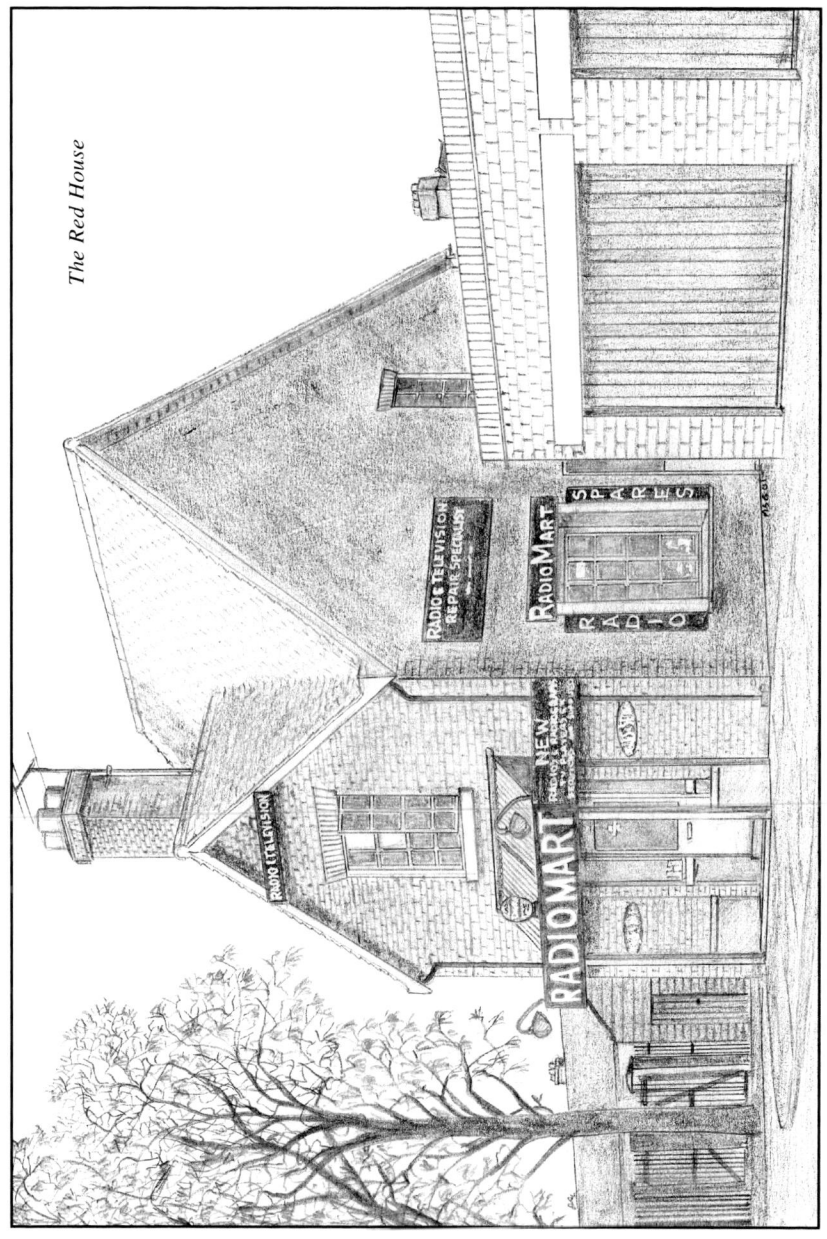

*The Red House*

local dealer to have it set up'. This was precisely what they did but unfortunately the catalogue never told them they would have to pay for the service!

When he first moved into the house the backroom was still used by Mitchell's as the estate office. The house itself was set at the southern end of an unused triangle of land which started at the junction of Chatsworth Avenue and Portsmouth Road. Across the apex of the triangle was a large advertising hoarding giving details of house prices on the new estate. What made it different was that the representations of the houses, instead of just being painted on, were built up in 3D which made it very eye catching.

Another interesting postscript was that when the house was modernised in the late 50's the chimneys were made lower and when the loft was being converted it was found to be thickly covered in straw. Was this one of the first forms of loft insulation?"

*Rosemary and Dan Curry*

A possible but I have to say, totally unsubstantiated explanation of the name Red House could be that this was the colour of Customs and Excise property at the time the house was built. Can any reader help? – Author.

## Pitreavie Road

Named after a town in Fife, Scotland, and has for many years been associated with the Royal Navy. In more recent times it has been the Maritime HQ, RN Signals. The road is residential only. It is part of the so called Dockyard Estate and the houses date from around 1930.

**Tudor Crescent**, after the Welsh connections with the Naval Estate. Henry Tudor, later King Henry VII was born in Pembroke in 1457.

There was an old fort which once stood where the Drill Hall now stands. Details are sketchy but from a sketch done by the City's historian of some 100 years ago, W. G. Gates, it appears to be basically an earth bank structure with military quarters within.

At the eastern end of the crescent where it joined the causeway along the northern side of the creek, is the Portscreek stormwater pumping station.

The most prominent building in the Crescent is the Army Drill Hall. It stands on the site which, during the building of the estate, was the bridgehead for materials being shipped in by barge. The site was operated by Frank Bevis and was known as the concrete depot.

Although WWII did not begin until 3rd September 1939 its inevitability was obvious to the 'powers that be' for several years prior to that date despite promises, assurances and things like Mr. Chamberlains' piece of paper. Various military installations began to sprout up around the country and one of Portsmouth's contributions to this was Tudor Crescent Drill Hall. Built in 1937 /38 and for the first part of the war became the RRHQ to the 57th Wessex Regt. (Artillery). Here they stayed until posted to North Africa.

Post war until 1967, the original roots were unearthed and it became 'home' to 457 Wessex Regt 'Q' Battery, HA RA TA (Heavy Artillery, Royal Artillery, Territorial Army). This unit was dedicated to the noble art of shooting down enemy aircraft.

*Waiting*

The business end of the unit consisted of two anti-aircraft (also suitable as anti-tank) guns originally of 1930's vintage. From memory we were told that they started life as 3.5" but over the years (including wartime use) had been up-rated to 3.7" with radar control. When in use they rested on the ground on a massive built in levelling platform whilst for transportation they were raised onto a set of four large road wheels with a self-contained towbar.

By the end of the 50's the towing vehicles were 5 ton Bedfords of which I believe the unit had four. The other towed vehicles were two radar trailers which were also fairly bulky pieces of equipment. The other vehicles which made up the battery's transport consisted of a huge 6-wheel recovery lorry – a Foden, I think; an Austin Champ (maybe two) which was the then up to date army's answer to the WWII jeep. Last and probably least, were the motorcycles– two 500cc BSAs and a 350cc Matchless of the late 40's vintage (the BSA's may have been earlier). These were used for the 'Don R's' which was army parlance for dispatch riders.

The building was not a lot different to what it is today except that there were a lot more outbuildings, mainly garages and workshops. In the roof of the hall was a "22 firing range. For "303 firing practice (this was the traditional British Army issue rifle for many of the preceding years) the troop had to go to the firing range at Browndown near Lee on Solent.

Two weeks each year saw the annual camp where you could put into practice what you had hopefully learned at the drill hall. The troop was split in two with the road party taking the guns and the rest of the equipment with enough men to drive, service and unload at the other end. The rest of the troop marched off to Cosham Railway Station carrying their kitbags where they embarked on a long boring train journey through the night to wherever. You were allowed to take your own transport but not many did.

The most common destinations were Sennybridge in the Brecon Beacons and Manorbier in Pembrokeshire although no doubt older gunners than myself will remember others. The whole was definitely an experience and gave us an insight (albeit a brief one) into the army life that lads of my age had just missed (luckily?) with the abolition of National Service.

*Author*

There was also an Army Cadet Force Unit attached to the drill hall complex. Their hut was at the eastern end of the area and from memory seemed to lead a life that was completely independent from the T.A. Its year of founding is not known exactly but it is mentioned in the City of Portsmouth Handbook of Youth (1947 Edition) from which I quote:

## ARMY CADET FORCE
## PORTSMOUTH

Meet at Tudor Drill Hall, Cosham, Portsmouth; Hilsea Drill Hall, Hilsea, Portsmouth; R.E. Drill Hall, Commercial Road, Portsmouth; Wessex Drill Hall, St. Pauls Road, Portsmouth. Ages for cadets; the cadet force is open to boys between 14 and 18 years. There are no fees and each boy is provided with a uniform.

Objects; to prepare boys through the medium of military training, technical instruction and comradeship to be leaders in both civilian and army life.

Officer Commanding; Lt. Col. D. O. d'E Miller, MC. Drill Hall, Commercial Road, Portsmouth.

"Around 1961 the Tudor Crescent ACF attracted some 30 lads. The unit was attached to 457 Anti-Aircraft Regt. which was also based there. The cadets, mainly in the 14–15 year age group were trained to parts 1 &

2 of the Regular Army Training Manual. The parade nights were Tuesday and Thursday with a club night on Saturday. As some of the lads were none too happy with their home life the latter proved very popular as indeed did the other nights as basically it kept them off the streets. Part of the training was rifle shooting with the basics being taught on the range over the top of the drill hall using "22 rifles. We had two Mossberg rifles which had six pack magazines and two Webleys which were single shot. When a certain proficiency level had been reached we progressed to the standard army issue "303 which we used at Browndown, Longmoor and at Winchester on the Royal Greenjackets' range.

Sunday saw us doing band practice. This was started at the suggestion of Major Lavender and Lt. Cannipel and we used the drill hall if it was available or the cadet hut if it wasn't. On occasions we used the parade square in the long defunct Hilsea Barracks. The band consisted of Drum Major, four side drums, one bass drum, two tenor drums and about ten bugles.

Reverting to the weapons, as a defence against the IRA (hardly anybody knew who they were at the time) our firearms had to be locked securely in our own armoury. The full count totalled WW1 vintage "303 Lee Enfields which were used for drill practice, two Bren Guns used for practice plus a fully serviceable one and the "22 rifles already mentioned.

We had annual camps at Shorncliffe in Kent, Tidworth on Salisbury Plain and Lulworth in Dorset. For these camps the whole of Hampshire cadet force was transported by troop trains laid on by British Rail. On top of this we had weekend camps at West Meon, Longmoor and with the Greenjackets at Winchester. Transport for these was provided by a 1 ton Morris Commercial army truck based at Tudor Crescent, a 5 ton Bedford borrowed from the T.A. and/or the Hants and IOW minibus.

As a bonus we also went with 457 Regt. T.A. for live practice anti-tank firing using their 3"7 guns on Salisbury Plain and also to Anglesea to witness live firings of the Thunderbird anti-aircraft missile.

Civilians were also admitted to the cadet hut in the form of two canteen girls, Yvonne and Kathleen.

"I think I got involved in it because I knew one of the boys who went there. All we had to do was to open the serving hatch and sell tea, coffee, lemonade and biscuits etc. I presume we washed up and tidied afterwards but it was a long time ago and I can't really remember."

*David Jelf and Yvonne*

A little known offshoot of the cadet force was a musical entertainment ensemble known as the Gatcombe Girls. This was a drum and bugle marching band with the entire troop dressed in drag. They were mainly cadets but with one or two T.A. members with a sense of humour joining in. The only time I saw them perform was at Moneyfields Sports and Social Club. They were billed as their title and very few people knew what they were in for. When they came out of their rather cramped dressing room and went straight into their routine, in the words of show business, 'They brought the house down'. To this day, I am sure with a good manager they could have 'gone places'.

*Author*

## Wembley Grove

No trace of a reason for this name. The only thing of note that I can find with this name is the national football stadium in London. It is not residential but just a 'joining' road. From Highbury Grove it continued as a track to the creek. On the left going towards the creek and immediately behind the Highbury houses was a small area of allotments. The other side of the track had a number of blackberry and hawthorn bushes and provided an alternative route onto Vosper's playing field. This track was swallowed up when Cliffdale School was built in the early 60's.

## Windsor Road

After the town or castle in Berkshire. Although not part of the estate it is included here due to its geographical location. Began in the last years of the 1800's but by 1908 had still only developed as far as the police station. It is a residential cul-de-sac although its eastern end is now connected to Hawthorn Crescent by a short alley and to the north of the railway by a footbridge.

*South Side*

| | |
|---|---|
| 20 | Mr. Eldridge, Boot Repairer |
| 34 | This was the old Cosham Police Station which stayed in use as such until 1952 when the present building was opened in Wayte Street. The old station stayed on in police hands for a few more years but as an accommodation centre only. It was eventually demolished and replaced by modern housing." In around 1937/ 38 I was stationed at Windsor Road police station. It was then somewhere around 40 years old and although occupied by the police it had three separate uses. The western end was used as private accommodation for the resident inspector whilst the remaining rooms upstairs and two downstairs were used for the 'living in' of the unmarried members of the force. The middle section downstairs was the bit of the station used by members of the public and for the administration of all the parts of the |

city on the mainland. The door on the left (see sketch) was a public entrance and behind the left window was the switchboard which, during the war, was in the able hands of a female member of the force. At the back of the building were three very substantial cells complete with shackles and ring bolts! Fortunately we had very little reason to use this accommodation and even when we had, the miscreants were soon moved to Fratton. During war a decontamination centre was built in the yard for any possible victims of mustard gas – fortunately it was never used.

For administration purposes five beat areas were set up and although the total area covered was large, the means of transport provided to cover it was limited to bicycles and feet. Being still fairly rural we came across a lot of stray animals of the farm variety as well as the normal cats and dogs. These had to be taken by us to a pound in what is now Wayte Street where the fire station stands. There was also a smaller pound in Windsor Road between that road (and belonging to) the railway although this was mainly used by local farmers when moving their livestock by rail. One of our duties was to keep our eye on the local fair which was an annual event on Portsdown Hill. We got extra pay for this duty plus the fact that we were always made welcome by the lady who ran the organisation. This welcome was often in the form of a nice warming toddy – strictly off the record of course!

When the station was built, it was under the control of the Hampshire Constabulary and this fact was carved in stone on the centre panel on the front of the building. This information was deemed of vital importance to the Germans in the event of an invasion and like all road signs was removed at the outbreak of war.

Windsor Road Police Station In 1922 when that station was taken under the Portsmouth police banner the police also doubled as firemen. To this end the Windsor Road premises was also the local fire station. Prior to this, the fire station was about half way up the High Street on the western side of the road.

Our fire engine was an old Ford with two ladders and possibly a pump on board. Fire alarms were raised using the Beasley-Gamewell system. Although we were always first on call for our area we always had a back up sent from the main station by the Guildhall.

The emergency was played out as follows; when the alarm went,

the driver would get the engine going and the nearest available man would join him. His sole job on the way to the fire was to ring the bell. On the way to the scene we would pick up fellow officers as we went up to a maximum crew of five. They were all numbered and had set duties to perform when we reached the scene of the fire. No1 connected the standpipe to the fire hydrant, No2 carried the key to turn the standpipe on; No3 connected the hose and was the first up the ladder, No4 had to help No3 and also get any messages back to HQ at the Guildhall, whilst last but not least, No5, had to look after the fire engine. The fire boxes eventually disappeared to be replaced by the more familiar blue police telephone boxes on their matching blue stands. Telephones both public and private were still a bit of a rarity even in the late 1930's and if you asked to use a private one the owner invariably asked if he would get paid for the call! It was a good area to work in and during the time I was there we had good times as well as bad. Probably the worst were the suicides but fortunately there were not many of them. The more amusing incidents concerned animals and these included chickens, goats, cows and horses. On one occasion chickens had been stolen from a local person and finished up (still alive) as a court case exhibit. Going on to horses, there was an incident of a youngish girl telling us of a horse that she had just left that was stuck in some mud on Farlington Marshes. Two of us accompanied her back to the marshes but by the time we got there it was dark. We had only our police flashlights and despite a long time searching we never found the poor creature. The girl could not remember exactly where she had seen it so we gave up and went home. Nothing more was heard so we assumed that it had managed to free itself and carried on with its life. This incident concerned one of the other Windsor Road officers and I was not involved. You didn't get many jobs like that in the city!

The Beasley-Gamewell System – this was the name of the fire alarm system in use in Portsmouth at the time. It consisted of red boxes on top of poles about 5'6" high. If a fire was discovered then you simply broke the glass and a signal was automatically sent back to the local station as well as the one at the Guildhall. This came through as a number punched into a card. The number represented an area in the city corresponding to where the box from where the alarm had been sent was situated. When the fire engine reached the firebox it had to be directed to the scene of the fire by the person who had set off the alarm (assuming he was still there). If, when you reached the fire, you needed to contact HQ then there was a means of communicating with them although again this used some form of code. One problem was that these boxes, like the telephones, were not at all prolific so sometimes you had a fairly long walk before you could make contact."

*Jim Pope (Superintendent Ret'd)*

68      Cosham College. Mr. Manvell was the principal of this rather grand sounding establishment which prepared pupils for Civil Service entrance exams.

72      National Deposit Approved Friendly Society

*North Side*

35      Humby Bros., Decorators

By 1956 all these enterprises had gone and the road was purely residential.

## Roads and Buses

The roads in the area appear to have been built after the houses. From what I have been told, Highbury and the 'joining' roads seem to have been metalled before the war and the same would seem to apply to the roads on the 'Dockyard Estate'. Chatsworth Avenue and Hawthorn Crescent did not get this treatment until after the war and Chats (as it was known to the younger generation) had to wait until the mid 50's to be completed. Hawthorn probably took preference over Chatsworth Avenue because of the prefabs that were built just after the war and this probably accounts for the bottom 50 or so yards of the latter. The majority of Chatsworth Avenue was different from the other roads as it was made of large concrete sections coloured pink whilst the others were just tarmac.

Apparently the estates' first bus service consisted of a seven seat limousine operated by the corporation before the war. This was followed by Bedford coaches but after the war the mainstay were double deck Daimlers with utility wartime bodies. These vehicles were renowned for their wooden slatted seats although a few were fitted with 'luxury' padded ones which had a sheet of brown 'plastic coated cloth' over a very thin padding fitted only to the bit of the seat you sat on. My grandfather always stood up when the bus went over the Cosham level crossing saying that 'It was a bally site more comfortable than sitting!' The service numbers were J and K and started from the top of the Wymering Estate. Once into Highbury they went down Chatsworth Avenue with a stop at every road junction, turned left into Wembley Grove, right into Hawthorn Crescent and continued into Highbury finishing by using the bottom of Chatsworth Avenue as a turning point. I think that the service was half hourly with about a quarter hour stopover at the end of each trip. As kids we got on well with the crews and often pestered them for any unused ticket rolls. It was a bit of a coup when we got one but for the life of me I cannot think what we actually did with it.

Other vehicles which were regular visitors to the estate were the bread vans, large milk lorries to replenish the milk floats in the middle of their round, lorries to empty the small pig swill bins, obviously the dustcarts and a mobile library.

# BITS AND PIECES

## Wartime

Several notable incidents all caused by bombing. Probably the most well known is the bombing of Highbury Buildings. This caused considerable damage to the centre of the block and the deaths of two sailors whose existence was not known until the wreckage was being cleared sometime later. Another bomb landed between Chatsworth Avenue and Hawthorn Crescent whilst at least two others, possibly incendiaries, landed in Highbury Grove and Pitreavie Road. As related elsewhere, there was an anti-aircraft gun at the end of Highbury Grove by the creek bank. If anyone can tell me any more wartime happenings I would be interested to hear from you.

## Road Names

As will have been seen, I have tried to give reason for the naming of the roads mentioned in this book but, as I will be the first to admit, not with a great deal of success. Road names are a fascinating subject in their own right. When trying to trace their origins there are two paths to go down to get an answer and they are quite simply 'what and why'? The first can be very easy or next to impossible to interpret, while the second, even if the first is known, can also be just about impossible to find out. I will try to illustrate the problems with some examples.

Nessus Street, Centaur Street and Hercules Street in our Old Buckland book. In classical Greek mythology, Nessus was the name of the Centaur who was killed by Hercules. Thus we know precisely who or what they were named after but why were three fairly nondescript Portsmouth streets so called?

Rowland Road and Raymond Road in Paulsgrove. Possibly men's names although the former usually does not include the 'w'. With these two we do not know either the what or the why.

Dovercourt Road and Wembley Grove. According to the story by William Stacey earlier in the this book, when the estate was being built the workforce were told that the roads were all to be named after famous houses. If this is true then where are (or were) the famous houses with these names?

Any help on this subject would be appreciated.

At this stage I will mention that Thomas Owen, a renowned Portsmouth architect, had his own house built in Kent Road, Southsea in 1848 and this was named Dovercourt. Why I do not know and whether there is any connection with the road of the same name in Highbury is also not known to me.

# POSTSCRIPT

After all the preceding had been prepared, I had the good fortune to watch a modern video made from an old film which was taken during the building of the Highbury Estate. This fascinating documentary gives an insight into just how labour intensive was the building trade at that period.

Mitchells' (the estate builders) yard was virtually a self contained complex with fairly substantial buildings as well as the traditional sheds. Virtually everything was made on site (the bricks were supplied by Bursledon Brickworks) with raw materials brought in by barge and landed by a very fit young man pushing a large fully loaded wheelbarrow up a rather narrow gangplank. Mechanisation was modest with small steam cranes, a narrow gauge railway and a mechanical navvy being the main candidates. Horses and carts were still in common use but by far the most common source of power was the human muscle!

On the creek bank just to the east of where the track extending from Wembley Grove joins it was a large corrugated iron building. This was there in the 50's and was the remains of the cement producing plant built during the estates' construction period. Outside was a large, round bowl – this was where the pug was mixed up. Shops appear to be trading (Carrolls') with the estate being built around them with the roads appearing to be low on the priority rating. The scenes remembered by William Stacey earlier in this book are all brought to life.

All in all this video is a fascinating piece of local history which can be obtained from the City Museum and Records Office.